# Shapes with Logan

Lorraine O'Garro

*Published by Melanin Origins LLC*
*PO Box 122123; Arlington, TX 76012*


*First Edition*



*Library of Congress Control Number: 2019909215*

*ISBN: 978-1-62676-661-7 hardback*
*ISBN: 978-1-62676-668-6 paperback*
*ISBN: 978-1-62676-667-9 ebook*

*Dedicated to Blue*

# Square

Window

# Triangle

Triangle

# Circle

# Swimming Pool

# Pentagon

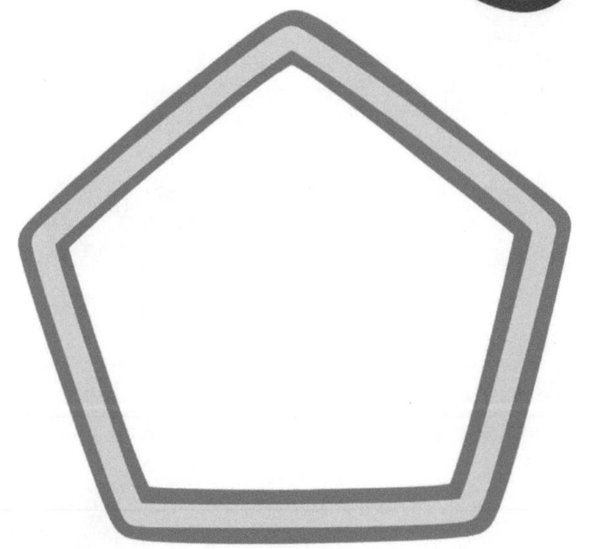

House

# Hexagon

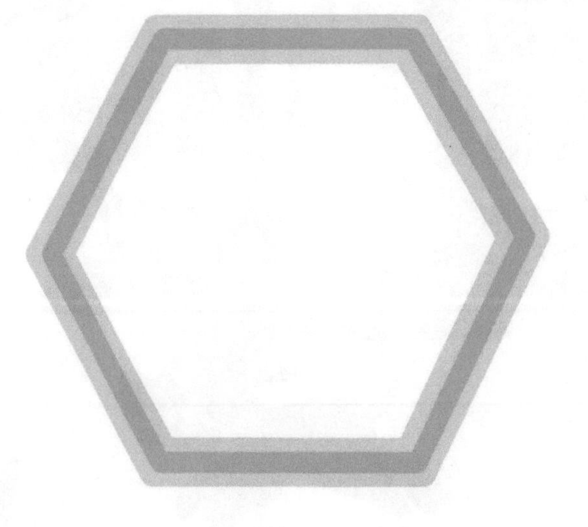

Beehive

# Octagon

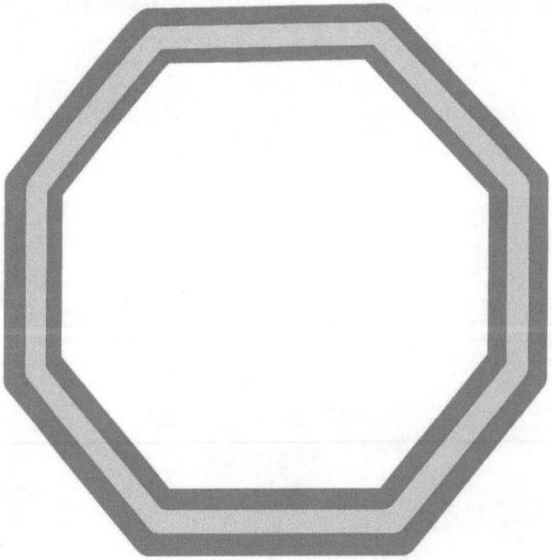

Clock

# Oval

Mirror

# Crescent

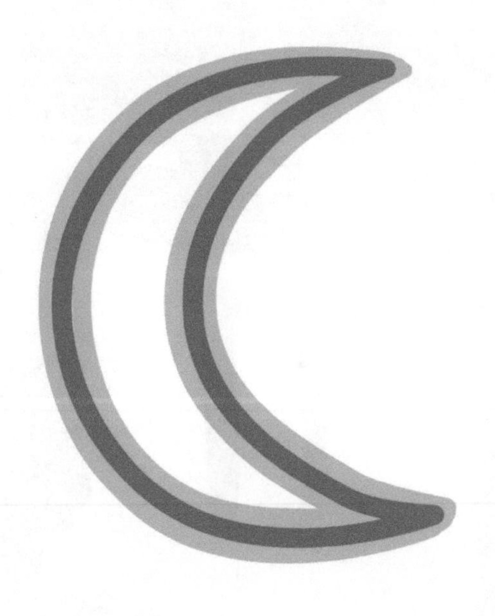

Moon

# Star

Starfish

Logan is the newest character to join Bella in her world adventures. To learn more with Bella visit learnwithbella.com

Lightning Source UK Ltd.
Milton Keynes UK
UKHW051144190520
363307UK00001BA/21
* 9 7 8 1 6 2 6 7 6 6 6 8 6 *